Prayers at Midpoint

Prayers at Midpoint

CONVERSATIONS WITH GOD FOR THOSE IN LIFE'S SECOND HALF

William A. Miller

AUGSBURG Publishing House • Minneapolis

To Marilyn

PRAYERS AT MIDPOINT
Conversations with God for Those in Life's Second Half

Copyright © 1983 William A. Miller

Scripture quotations unless otherwise noted are from Holy Bible: New International Version. Copyright 1978 by the New York International Bible Society. Used by permission of Zondervan Bible Publishers.

Photos: Strix Pix, 10, 81; Jim Solheim, 19; Paul M. Schrock, 30; Paul Conklin, 45; Rohn Engh, 56.

Library of Congress Cataloging in Publication Data

Miller, William A., 1931-
   PRAYERS AT MIDPOINT.

   1. Prayers   I. Title.
BV245.M53 1984   242   83-72110
ISBN 0-8066-2054-4

Manufactured in the U.S.A.   APH 10-5081

1 2 3 4 5 6 7 8 9 0 1 2 3 4 5 6 7 8 9

Contents

Preface

Prayer is a privilege granted to everyone who believes in God. It is a divine gift; an opportunity to converse with the Almighty. Prayer is the channel, the pathway from the innermost core of a human being to the presence of the Creator.

But while we may talk about prayer and even discuss it at great length, it is only by praying that we realize what prayer is. Only the experience itself can give true definition to prayer.

This is a book about prayer, therefore, because it is a book *of* prayers. They are communications to a hearing and listening Father. We take our cue from Martin Luther, who said that in the phrase, "Our Father, who art in heaven," God encourages us to believe that he is truly our Father, and we are his children. Therefore we are to pray to him with complete confidence, just as children speak to their loving father. We open our innermost selves to God in our prayers with the same boldness, confidence, and vulnerability that we displayed when we rushed into the trustworthy arms of our earthly parents.

Boldly, confidently, and with great vulnerability: that is the way we pray; and that is particularly the case with this volume of prayers. Since they focus on that special age of mid-life, they demand boldness and confidence. They require the opening up of the innermost self. On the one hand they are very personal prayers; yet on the other they belong to everyone journeying on the pilgrimage through the midyears of life. They reflect the issues of that age: identity, mortality, fulfillment, uncertainty, authority. They reflect the ambiguities, inconsistencies, and opposites as well as the certitude, maturity, and great potential of mid-life.

Therefore in these prayers readers will find the heights of joy and the depths of sadness, casual informality and profound respect, agony and ecstasy, exasperation, humor, anger, grief, gratitude, regret, depression, delight, frustration, and reward. The prayers may sometimes seem disjointed, but they are typical of the real feelings experienced in mid-life.

Prayers do not necessarily provide answers or solutions to the quandries and the turmoil of our lives. Sometimes in these outpourings of our hearts we are able to come to new insights simply by verbalizing our deepest feelings. But just as often, we end a prayer feeling just as uncertain as when we began. We are compelled to return again . . . and again . . . and again.

It is fascinating territory, this midpoint of life. We are no longer young, but not yet old. We have learned enough to know that we really know very little. And we have finally "made it" only to find ourselves once again wondering who we are and what it's all about. The journey into the second half of life brings both excitement and dread, and we can use all the help we can get.

Prayer stands ready!

Why Is Life More Complicated?

Life never used to be so complicated, Lord, at least not as I remember it. There was a certain simpleness that left me with more time to myself. And now it seems like there's so much more that has to be done. There weren't nearly as many demands or as many decisions to be made. I don't recall that the pace was any slower, but I do know that my spectrum of involvement in life was a lot narrower than it is now. A *lot* narrower.

Maybe that's what it's all about. That involved a decision or I guess a host of decisions that I made through the years. I've noticed lately that I like to say my life seems more and more to be lived *for* me (as though I had no control). I come off sounding like a martyr.

I'll bet you are smiling at that one—maybe even chuckling.

Well, I have to smile myself. I know that the complications are there largely by my choice. And I admit no real regrets. I have chosen and continue to choose to pursue life rather than just to live it. The abundance of life that you told me about is certainly very real, and I like it.

But I do need some help in making decisions. I need the wisdom of foresight and the common sense to keep a balance.

And when I have made my decisions, give me your grace to live with the consequences—good or evil.

Amen.

My God, How Full of Wonder You Are!

My God, how full of wonder you are!

Much of the time I am running so busily through life that I miss you, but regularly I run smack into you. And each time it happens I can do nothing but stand back in awe at your splendor, and worship your might, your power, your majesty. I know you are beyond the powers of my mind but I am compelled to say it, to affirm it: "You are indeed God Almighty."

I think for too long *Almighty* was only a word; a religious word yes, but a word lacking magnitude in my perception. It is only through these continued encounters in the living of my years that I even begin to approach an awareness of the majesty and the omnipotence that is yours. I can hardly contemplate you without my mind being blown open. To think—to *think* of your creativity, I stagger in my mind. To imagine even in my wildest fantasy how you have gone about and do go about your endless creating, overloads my limited powers, and I am overwhelmed with awe.

But that isn't all. There is always a great magnetism to this. And I feel drawn to you. You—Creator of galaxies unnumbered—and I—a speck of your creation. Could there be a greater contrast?

And the magnetism prevails. And I feel your love. And I love you.

My God, how full of wonder you are!
Amen.

I Need a Balance between "Old" and "Young"

I just read that some pollster discovered people in mid-life tend to think of themselves as younger in years than they are. So?! Is there something wrong with that? What's the point of thinking you are a decrepit has-been when you're actually cresting towards the zenith of your life? Start thinking "old" and pretty soon you're creaking.

But I have to laugh when I hear myself say that because I can hear the irritation and the defensiveness in it. I know that little piece of information has penetrated a sensitive zone. No doubt it's true that there isn't anything "wrong" with thinking of myself as younger in years than I am, but I still continue to try to *do* what I did 20 years ago, and sometimes that can turn out to be disastrous.

Help me to balance it, Lord. Help me to get a balance between the extremes of thinking I'm still a 25-year-old on the one hand and a crotchety old duffer on the other. Help me to be realistic about what my body can and cannot do at this point in my life. I don't like to own the limitations that I begin to experience, but while I may continue to challenge myself, help me also to sensibly take care of myself. And give me the grace, please, to focus on what I *can* do.

Amen.

I Think I'm Slipping

I think I'm slipping. I wonder if I *am* slipping? Nobody has told me that I am. But then again nobody has told me that I'm not.

What do you think about the poster that says, "Just because you're paranoid doesn't mean they're not out to get you"? It's probably nonsense, huh?

Well I don't know, Lord. Maybe I've passed my prime and peaked out. Maybe it's all downhill from here on. Maybe I should have stayed in engineering. I don't know. I think I used to do a better job than I do now. It seemed before that I somehow made a difference in the lives of people. Maybe that's gone.

I think my colleagues are doing a better job than I am. They seem to get approval. Not that that is everything, but it's something.

Maybe I ought to try something else. Maybe I ought to go to one of those career assessment centers and see if I need a mid-life career change.

It sure is a rotten day, Lord.

Amen.

I Feel Close to You, God

The gentle waves lap the hull of the sailboat. It's a soothing sound, Lord, and I've come to cherish it as a kind of therapy—sort of a healing medicine. And the sun too—warm on my skin, encouraging me to relax, to drowse, to drift into fantasy. The planks of the dock are hard against my back and head, but they are a strong support and I can let my weight sink onto them.

It's not much, I guess. Not really. Lying on a dock, sun, water gurgling around a boat hull. But it just seems to make me feel close to you. And I like that.

My God, you are good to me.

Amen.

I Value Our Conversations

It occurred to me that I take time to think of you more often than I used to. It occurred to me that my conversations with you are a lot more frequent than before. It occurred to me that many more of my experiences provoke my talking with you. I seem to slip into conversation with you more frequently, more naturally, more intensely, as though you were a constant companion, ever ready to converse; which is, of course, precisely what you are.

Sights and sounds move me to think of you. Memories and experiences prompt me to talk to you. In the midst of maddening traffic or atop a snowy mountain, it happens. In the reverence of your house or among noisy crowds, it happens. In pain or need or in joy or fullness, it happens. In my romanticism and sentimentality I feel your closeness and your warmth. But I feel it no less when I rave on with anger and resentment or behave like a spoiled child. In my anguish I feel your support, but it is no less when I pour out my gratitude for your goodness and mercy.

As long as I can remember, I have known all this to be true. But somehow, of late it has had new meaning, new depth. It is more important, more valuable than ever before. I need it, and you provide it.

O God, I thank you.

Amen.

Is My Fuse Growing Shorter?

Tell me, do I have a shorter fuse than most people? I mean, do I have a quicker temper? Do I get mad faster? Does it take less to set me off? Am I abnormal?

Or did I get blessed with a kid who has the uncanny skill to light my fuse and explode my dynamite?

Why does he have to be so stubborn? Where did he get such a will? Why don't you show him the light or something?

Arrgh-h-h!

Thank you for listening, God.

Amen.

I Like to Think I'm Still Out in Front

I saw a little desk motto the other day that read, "Don't look back; they may be gaining on you." Whoever coined that one surely knew what he or she was talking about. Most of the time I like to think that I'm still out in front, but maybe I'm only kidding myself thinking that I'm going to stay there. A younger generation is hot on my tail, and sometimes I get the feeling that they are breathing down my neck. I don't think I'm afraid of competition, but maybe I am. Is there really anything to that business of nobody wanting you after you're 50? How vulnerable should I allow myself to be? If I become a mentor do I risk being replaced? Am I being realistic in assessing my security, or is this the beginning of paranoia?

I certainly do seem to have an awful lot of questions today, Lord. I hope that's natural.

Amen.

There Is an Urge to Run Away

I wonder what would happen, Lord, if I just kept on driving this morning? I wonder what would happen if I just ran away?

You know, a lot of people do that. They just "disappear." They start out for work in the morning, just as they have done thousands of other times; but instead of turning off the freeway at their exit, they just keep on driving and "disappear."

You have to admit it has its appeal, Lord. No doubt about that. I'm a responsible worker, a responsible spouse, a responsible parent. I wonder what would happen if I were ever irresponsible? I wonder if it would be any easier? Fewer hassles? Less stress? Not so many demands and expectations?

Have you ever had that urge, Lord—just to run away from it all?

Amen.

You Love and Accept Me As I Am

It dawns on me again, Lord, that you are ready and willing to love me and accept me as I am.

I know that. I've known it for many years now. But I still think I have to make it myself. I'm not sure I really know *how,* or what "it" is that I think I have to make, but that doesn't seem to matter or make any difference. I still feel the push to perform, the stress to shape up, the demand to do things right. I've learned it well—so well that I can even quarrel with myself about the foolishness of it all and continue to lose the argument. Oh, not all the time, mind you. There *are* those rare times of abandon— those hours or days of letting go. But I have learned it so well—the performance pattern—that it's extremely difficult to break out of it, and I sometimes wonder if I even want to.

What am I going to do? Will you help me? Help me to accept your grace. I said I've got it in my head; I don't need any more learning. I need help to risk letting go. I know the earth is not going to cease orbiting if I relax in my compulsion. I need help to take the chance, to make the leap.

I need *your* help. Please.

Amen.

The Need to Please Is Less

I had an interesting experience today, Lord. It dawned on me that I am not nearly as concerned about winning other people's approval as I used to be. I was talking with a fellow who didn't seem to agree with the approach I was suggesting. In fact he left *disagreeing* with me, and I found myself saying to myself, "Well, I guess that's okay."

Maybe there's nothing particularly special about this, but then again, maybe there is. I had the good feeling of being aware that I didn't need to please him so he would like me and accept me. I wouldn't say that I used to be a people-pleaser, but I certainly have always been conscious of people's opinions of me. And I certainly have wanted them to think well of me. But somehow today that just wasn't as important.

This is a strange experience, Lord, because I still want people to accept me and think well of me, but today it wasn't somehow as important to me whether that fellow agreed with me or not. I felt confident in my approach and didn't see any need to change it in order to please him. I felt secure in my own assessment of myself and I didn't have to depend on his.

This is a great feeling, Lord.
Amen.

It Would Be So Easy Just to Go Crazy

I joke about it, but I mean it, God. It would be so very, very easy just to go crazy. I tell you the pressures are tremendous. I no more get one issue settled than two more are on top of me. This one wants this; that one wants that. Demands. Expectations. Needs. Deadlines. "Get it done." "Help me." "Hurry up." "I need it."

Who said you don't allow more to fall on us than we're able to bear?

I seriously want you to know that going crazy wouldn't take any effort at all. In fact it would be a welcome relief to get away from all this pressure in whatever way I could. They can call it escape from reality or some technical name or whatever anyone chooses. Just to get out from under the responsibility. To slip quietly into another realm. Let someone take care of *me!*

How am I going to make it? I don't know if I can. Hold onto me. Please.

Amen.

A Sense of Humor Saved Me Again

O God, what is more salvific than a sense of humor? (I suppose you know what that word means. I heard someone use it the other day. He said it means "productive of salvation.")

I certainly don't mean to get into a theological discussion. I just mean that having a sense of humor has saved me from the pits more than once. And it happened again today, so I thought I'd say thanks to you for a sense of humor.

Maybe this is one of the benefits of middle age. I don't recall being able to chuckle at myself so freely in my earlier years. (I must have been more uptight then.) But whatever, it *is* rather helpful to be able not to take life quite so seriously. I don't want to become a slough-off or a nerd, mind you, but I like to be able to laugh quietly at my foolishness and foibles and to shake my head gently at myself and to go on.

Do *you* do it? I mean, are *you* somehow responsible for that happening? Do you make a neuron fire somewhere in my brain to break up the pattern? Or how does it work?

You know I had been in the pits of self-doubt and sliding self-confidence—for no real reason. In fact *now* I don't even know how I got into that rut. But today it was as if someone changed my channels, and I listened to myself and started to laugh at what I heard me saying. What nonsense!

How did it happen? How come today I see me differently than I saw me yesterday? *Do* you make neurons fire that cause such occurrences? How can I understand this? Can I? Or is it destined to remain a mystery?

I don't know. All I know is the sense of humor saved me again. And however it comes about, I rejoice in it and thank you, God.

Amen.

I Don't Like Growing Old

I was reminded again today, Lord, that I'm not as young as I used to be. That is a painful reminder, and frankly, I don't like it. I resent growing old.

That may not make much sense, but it really doesn't matter. That is the way I *feel*.

I'm not alone either. Why do you think everyone wants to live longer, but no one wants to grow old?

I'll tell you why. It's no fun.

I just am not able to do what I used to be able to do. And I don't like those limitations.

I suspect that sounds arrogant, that I really don't have control over this aging business. I'm angry because I don't, particularly when I think I ought to.

Well, I'm sorry if that's the way it sounds, but I'm not about to accept this thing without letting you know how I feel. There ought to be a better way. Why do I *have* to run out of energy more quickly than before? Why do I *have* to tire sooner than I used to? Why *must* it take longer now for me to rejuvenate? Why can't my body keep up with my mind?

Those are hard questions, Lord. Where are the answers?

Amen.

You Certainly Are a Master of Timing

You touched me again today, Lord. In the midst of my self-pity you visited me in the form of another who shared wounds so like my own it was uncanny. This was a person much stronger than I—someone who risked opening heart and soul, who sought nothing more from me than a listening ear and an attentive eye, and whose unburdening of self provided me with insight of my own. Oh, how I needed that! How I needed that today.

You knew it, didn't you? It wasn't mere chance, was it? It might have happened yesterday or tomorrow, but it didn't. I marvel at your timing, Lord. Truly, "there is a time for everything, and a season for every activity under heaven."

Thank you.

Amen.

How I Relish the Blessing of Grace!

What would I do without your grace? Would I make it through even another day? I doubt it. The cost would be too high—I would have to be perfect. And, much as I would rather not admit it, the truth is, Lord, I am *not* perfect.

You *know* that, don't you? Even I have to chuckle to myself on that one. I have grown dependent on your grace, and the older I get, Lord, the clearer that is. I don't know if it's because of the adding up of years, or if it's some other factor. All I know is that your grace and mercy are continually more real in my life than ever before. Your grace seems to be my constant companion whether I think of it or not. It surrounds me and fills me. It permeates the "business" of my daily life. It is quietly omnipresent in my realm.

I do not understand it, but I know it is real. I do not understand *how* you can continue to show me grace in your uninterrupted acceptance of me, even when I know you are deeply pained by my repeated failures. That is simply beyond me. It is overwhelming.

But I thank you for it. Dear God, I thank you for it. I do not need to understand it to know it is real.

I only need to let it be.

Amen.

I Am Tired of Hearing People Complain

Dear God, I get so tired of hearing people complain. They make mountains out of molehills, court cases out of petty annoyances, tragedies out of minor losses, melodramas out of everyday aggravations. They all exaggerate. They inevitably feel abused, taken advantage of, and martyred. They are always innocent, faultless, and pure as the driven snow.

Yech!

I would like to tell them to shut up, get lost, buzz off. I would like to tell them that they make me sick with their incessant bellyaching. I would like to tell them they are paranoid. I would like to take them by the hand and show them what *real* trouble looks like.

Why can't they realize that they cannot everlastingly have their own way? Why can't they finally abandon their infantile egocentricity? Why can't they accept the fact that life as we know it has its ups and downs, its pluses and minuses, its forwards and reverses, *and there is really not a lot that anybody can do about it!* They are enough to drive a person mad!

Love the unlovable? Well, I'll tell you, it's pretty hard to love *them*. I sometimes wonder how you do it.

Amen.

I Am Sorry for My Arrogance

I approach you in deep humility, Lord God. I apologize for my arrogance and my rudeness. I thank you that you have created me as a special person of great worth and value. But I go beyond that. I get caught up in my own wisdom and sophistication and conveniently forget about your counsel. I become enamored by my schemes and visions, and willfully violate what I know is your will and your wish for me. I fly in the face of our relationship and behave more rudely to you, Almighty God, than perhaps even to fellow mortals. Sometimes I cannot believe how much I separate myself from you. I am truly sorry. Amen.

Pain Is a Very Private Thing

Pain is a very private thing. I really can't give it over to anyone else, and no other person can ever know what my pain is actually like. I know some people who say give it up to Jesus, but I don't think I even know what that means, Lord.

People will say they understand, but they don't understand. So what is the point? Why should I share my pain with someone when the person doesn't understand? Why should I risk more pain? Why take the chance that they might laugh at me, or chastise me, or make me feel guilty, or tell me, "Listen, I complained that I had no shoes, until I met a man who had no feet."

Pain is a very private thing. So I don't go around telling people my anguish. I don't expose my shattered, broken heart and mind and spirit. I don't tell them how torn up and bleeding I am or how many times I think I have already died from the intensity of the pain. I don't confess how out of control I am and how vulnerable I feel, because they just don't know what I'm talking about.

Sometimes I don't know if even you understand, Lord. Do you? You must. You have to! There's no other place. Will you hear me and accept me and love me in my wretchedness?

Amen.

I Celebrate the Joy of Parenthood

I got choked up with deep feelings of love for our children today. One son had a birthday—number 21 —and I wrote him a special note. I told him how deeply we loved him, how proud we were of him, what potential for a great future lay ahead of him and how we hoped he would seize it. I gave him the note, across the table, when we began the celebration. When he read it, he looked at me. And in that one instant, Lord, volumes passed between us in utter silence.

You wonder. Often as a parent you wonder how it's all going to turn out. You hope and you pray and you do what you think is best, and of course you never really know if it's best or not. It's a tough, demanding job, and there's never any guarantee that your heart isn't going to get broken in the end.

But what a joy on a day like today. What a delight! All the agonies are forgotten and the ecstasy of deep love is supreme. You give us this joy, Lord; it is *your* love within us that we share with each other. You give us this joy, Lord, and I thank you.

Amen.

There Are Thoughts in My Head about Dying

I have become aware that every once in a while
I find myself thinking about dying.
I didn't used to do that, Lord.
I guess that's okay.
Amen.

You Fill My Life with Surprises

You seem never to allow my life to become boring —at least not for very long. Maybe you have a giant salt shaker of sorts, packed with surprises that you generously sprinkle over the days of my life. I don't know whether you are responsible or not for all the goings on that occur, and I have absolutely no desire to get into a theological debate about whether you cause stuff or allow stuff or use stuff. All I know, God, is that it certainly seems to me that there are a lot of surprises in my life, and I am convinced that you have a hand in them.

They're not all pleasant, those surprises, but even the most painful seem to have something about them that link me to you, once I have worked through my myriad of feelings. The shock, the disbelief, the rage that this "surprise" could even be happening, somehow in my own time, pass on. I become aware that through it all you haven't let go, and I am still firmly hooked onto you.

But those pleasant surprises, like pieces of sun dancing on rippling waters or diamond crystals sparkling in the snow; oh, God, how they lift my soul and thrill it! Big ones and little ones drop in when least expected and pop up in the oddest places. But that's the way surprises are, isn't it?

Thank you for surprises.

Amen.

Your Word Means So Much to Me

I remembered today how I used to read the Bible when I was a kid. It was a big, old King James Version, and I used to read it every morning. Actually, I was reminiscing with a friend, and he mentioned that in his house they had a Bible in their bathroom, and he remembers as a kid reading it every morning.

I'm glad we had that big, old King James, Lord. I'm glad I read it. I guess I'll never really forget what I read in that Bible day after day, and I doubt that anyone will ever be able to take it away from me. It means more to me than I suspect I ever thought it would.

Maybe it was just habit; I don't know. Maybe it was sincere inner motivation. But whatever, I am convinced that what I read became a firm part of the foundation for all of my life. And I thank you, God. I thank you for that experience and the consequences of it.

Amen.

Death Is an Alien; It Doesn't Belong

I was talking to a man today who has a terminal disease. He is going to die. He knows it, but he gives the impression that he isn't too upset by it.

I got to thinking, Lord. I suspect I would be pretty upset if I knew I was going to die. I would be mostly angry. I would be angry with you. Not that that would make any real sense. But that is neither here nor there, because logic does not enter into this matter.

I know theology. I understand death in the Christian context. And death is certainly no stranger to me. But God, at this point in my life I say it's just not fair; death is just not fair. People can rationalize it and justify it till doomsday and it doesn't change a thing; it doesn't make death okay. Death is alien; it is an enemy; it doesn't belong.

That's why I will be angry.

Amen.

Your Love and Respect Amaze Me

Your love is almost too good to be true. At least, the way I *perceive* it, your love is almost too good to be true. The fact that you continue to love me *no matter what* sometimes blows my mind away. That is simply too good to be true.

And so I doubt. I say, "No! God's love could not *possibly* extend to me as I am now. I must be outside God's love. No one could *truly* love me. Not now. Not even God!"

That's dumb, isn't it? Dumb and egomaniacal. I guess that turns out to be a rather neat power play, doesn't it? I am so unlovable that even you, Almighty God, creator of vast galaxies, cannot love me. I end up thinking I have more control and power than you. Yes, that *is* egomaniacal—and dumb. It must be rather humorous to you.

I'm sure it is.

But you never laugh at me, do you? You respect me too much ever to do that. You love me too much ever to do that.

Oh, my God, you are too wonderful for me.

Amen.

How Wonderful Are Your Gifts!

This evening a woman asked me, "How did you come to be so smart?" And she genuinely meant it. She wasn't trying to be smart or sarcastic.

I said, "I don't know. Maybe it was in the genes I got from my father; he was pretty smart and talented." And I let it go at that.

Well, I don't know if that's right or not, Lord. Possibly. But I don't really believe that our talents are due to chance genetics. You sprinkle your blessings and gifts over all of us, and you don't miss anyone. And we may choose to use and develop those gifts or choose to let them sit idle.

Thank you for the gifts, Lord. And thank you for the motivation.

Amen.

The Clods Are Gaining on Us

Why did you make so many clods? It is absolutely infuriating! They drive vehicles as if they were under anesthesia. They give service as if they were all green trainees. The words *responsibility* and *reliability* are foreign to their brains. The ancient psalmists used to pound at your door screaming about the heathen seeking to do them in. It's not the heathen; it's the clods.

You're absolutely right! When this world comes to an end it isn't going to be by flooding or by holocaust or whatever. We're going to be done in by the clods—by ineptitude, by incompetence, by irresponsibility, by sloth, and by sloppiness.

They're everywhere, God. And I've just about had it!

Amen.

My Life Is More Than I Ever Expected

It is amazing to me how many new insights make their way into my mind these days. Is that another aspect of this mid-life experience, Lord? It's not that I have been unaware or out of touch in times past; it's just that it appears to me that I realize things more often now—things make sense more regularly than ever before in my life.

They certainly are not all pleasant, positive insights, but many of them are. And those that aren't seem to have their own way of helping me understand more of myself and what is going on in my life.

I have become aware of how much more full my life has been than I ever expected it to be. You remember how I used to dream and fantasize about my future. But those were only dreams and fantasies— or so I thought. Actually I have experienced more successes and failures than I ever dreamed I would. There has been a lot more pain and anguish as well as greater joys and thrills than I thought there would be. But most of all there has been a depth to my experience of life that I could not ever have imagined even in my wildest fantasy.

And who can say, Lord, what is yet to come? Should I have any reason to expect that the days of my life shall be any less full in the future? Hardly. But while that is exciting to contemplate, it is frightening as well. Still I feel confident, Lord; I feel confident and good.

Amen.

Thank You for Our Intimate Family

You know there is a very deep sense of love running through our little family. And you already know how grateful I am for that. But I want to tell you anyway, because in my telling you about it, the love means even more.

The love was, of course, your idea in the first place. I doubt very much that we would have thought it up on our own. But you told us about it, and you showed it to us, and you taught us how to go about giving to one another what we had received from you.

I thank you for this intimate little family. You are indeed a giver of good gifts.

Amen.

Will I Ever Know Satisfaction?

What *is* satisfaction, Lord? Is it some kind of median between contentment and ambition? And what about striving on the one hand and relaxing on the other? Is satisfaction somewhere in between these?

I'm not sure I even know what this is all about or where it's coming from. It's just that I get troubled over this business of satisfaction, wondering if I ever will be truly satisfied and then wondering if I *want* to be. Is satisfaction a goal that I want to strive for or is it something that I want to avoid? Not that dissatisfaction is desirable, mind you, but maybe satisfaction mesmerizes a person so that he or she who is fully satisfied doesn't have any more frontiers.

I seem to want to keep pushing out the boundaries of my experience of life. But I also know I want the good feeling of contentment. Please help me find the balance.

Amen.

I'm Not the Person I Used to Be

This is probably going to sound trite, Lord, but I'm not the person I used to be. Whether I think that is good or bad is neither here nor there. I'm just a little concerned. Change is nice, but so is the comfort of status quo.

I don't recall particularly wanting or requesting this experience, but I'm not saying that I want to reject it either. It feels a little strange, I guess, and I'm not exactly sure what is going on.

Some things that used to be important to me are no longer all that important. Then again, I have become increasingly aware of how much certain things mean to me, when before I could either take them or leave them. For some time now I have found myself interested in matters that were of little interest to me before. I have even found myself viewing events and experiences with a different kind of attitude—a different kind of evaluation.

I *am* different, or I am becoming different. Somehow I'm changing. In a way I like that, but in a way I don't. Sometimes I wish I would stay the way I was; yet other times I can hardly wait to see what is going to happen in me next. It is an upsetting and yet affirming experience—strange but assuring.

Be my constant, Lord. Be my constant in the midst of these variables. Be my "old and sure" in the face of so much new and untried. Be the changeless one you are, my confidence and my certitude.

Amen.

Deliver Me from the Advice Givers

O God, deliver me from the advice givers. They are such a pain in the neck. You are reported to have said, "It is more blessed to give than to receive." And while I don't think you meant the "it" to be *advice,* it certainly does fit. And there are legions of people who daily testify to that.

They drive me absolutely crazy. Even before I fully explain a problem, they have a solution well in hand. Even before the issue has been identified, they know the answer. They have an answer for anything. No, they have an answer for *everything*—even answers they don't know they have, even solutions to unpresented problems.

And they are so gracious and generous with their "wisdom." They will give it freely even when unsolicited. They always know exactly how I feel. They always have been through precisely what I'm going through. And they are driven, maybe even obsessed, with telling me what I should, ought, and must do so that everything will turn out just fine.

O God, deliver me from the advice givers.

Amen.

Am I in "Adolescence Revisited"?

I'm beginning to believe I'm in a sort of "adolescence revisited" zone. I read something about that not too long ago—someone wrote that there are a lot of similarities between the adolescent years and the mid-life years.

Frankly, that observation *could* be upsetting because, as I remember, living through that time was not exactly a piece of cake. While we were certainly having a lot of fun in those years, most of us were struggling through matters of personal identity, vocational choice, human relationships, and other magnanimous issues. Oh, yes, we made it alright, but not without a fair share of anxiety and anguish.

On the other hand, there's a dimension of warmth to this comparison that actually is rather supportive for me. Maybe I'm caught in remembering only what I want to remember and forgetting what is too painful to recall, but my recollection of adolescence is one of fond memories with more smiles than tears. I had difficult days by all means—but my adolescence was a challenging time of exploration and discovery, of being open to learning, of profound changes, of seeking identity.

This gives me a confidence, God, a kind of surety that even though I made my share of mistakes getting through adolescence, I remember it as a very exciting time. Why then shouldn't I find these similar years of mid-life to be just as rich?

Amen.

I'm Struggling for a Sense of Direction

Here I am, Lord, having lived more years than I probably have yet to live, and I still don't really know what I want to be when I grow up. That may very well sound humorous, but I think I really mean it. Maybe that's my way of trying to lighten something that is heavier than I like to think it is.

I'm not exactly sure I'm dissatisfied with what I am now. At least I don't see myself tearing around seeking to be something else. Still, there's a certain degree of stagnation about my life, and there doesn't seem to be any place to go up.

Is this peculiar, Lord? Not too long ago I read a survey that indicated a vast majority of people are quite content doing what they're doing. However, I also hear about people who just quit doing what they are doing and go off and do something else.

Maybe I've lost my sense of direction; is that what it's all about? It's hard to say. I certainly don't feel as though I'm lost at sea. But on the other hand, I don't think my course is as certain as it once was.

Can you give me any direction, Lord? I'll take all the help I can get.

Amen.

Is Anything More Powerful Than Love?

I think of love, and it is good. I think of love, and it is painful. And I ask you, how can one such thing so totally run the gamut of human feeling and experience as to generate both absolute ecstasy and excruciating anguish?

Tell me, do we simply not have the capacity to probe and know the depth of things like love until we've reached this point of having already lived longer than we have yet to live? Is it our destiny that most of us shall simply skip around on the surface and slip along in relative naivete about the magnitude and the depth of love until we have already spent more years than we have left to spend?

I have heard people say, "Love is wasted on the young." I wonder if there isn't some truth to that. At first we believe love is a gleeful spree. We look at love with rosy idealism, never seeing or never wanting to see its shadow, and our experience is only incomplete. But with the accumulation of years the opposites emerge, and we slowly or suddenly see the bittersweetness that gives love its incredible magnitude and magnetism.

O God, whether I be swept to heights of indescribable ecstasy or crushed in the anguish of misery, let me know the fullness, the breadth, and the depth of love. By your mercy may there be at least a balance between the happiness and the hurt, the pleasure and the pain, and I shall be fulfilled.

Amen.

It's Hard to Let Them Leave the Nest

Another one has "left the nest." I wonder again how well prepared he is. Is he ready? How will he make it? *Will* he make it?

It is sometimes rather amusing, Lord, how I get into conversation with myself about this. It doesn't quite reach the point of argument, but it gets pretty close. I throw up one of these "wonderments" and then I counter that with "Yes, but don't forget this." Such a counter doesn't help all that much, though, primarily because I want to keep my doubts, so I challenge myself with a new question. And then I come up with a response that attempts to reassure me and encourage me to quit worrying. Not that I worry, because I really don't believe I do. But then again, maybe I do.

Could you tell me, why does letting kids go have to be one of the toughest responsibilities of parenthood?

Whatever . . . thank you for faith.

Amen.

I Have to Do Some Planning

I have to do some planning. If I don't sit down and take some time to begin to map things out, my life is going to run away with me. The days are flying by faster and faster, so if I don't do this soon there won't be anything left to plan.

It's obvious to me that this is no easy task. It requires some discipline, and that in itself is reason enough for procrastination. It is one thing to want to be able to do something, but it is altogether a different matter to sit down and plan it out.

You know very well that I haven't lived my life this way. I'm not saying I've never made plans. Of course I have made plans. But planning has not been my usual way. Maybe if it had been I would be better off today than I am. In fact I probably would.

But whether that is true or not, the fact remains that I have to, no, I *want* to change my pattern and make some concrete plans for the next several years. It's important to me; I truly want to do it. Please help me fight procrastination!

Amen.

It's Good to Be among People

I like people. By and large people are okay. I realize that you took quite a risk making people, but I think that more often than not it has paid off positively. Of course there are some especially notable exceptions to that generalization (as you well know), but still, it was a good idea.

Would you do it all over again? I mean, if you had it to do over again, would you create us? Does the joy you get from people outweigh and outdistance the anguish and the agony? That's a hard one to answer, isn't it? But I'd be willing to bet that it does. You are pleased and you are satisfied with the small joys, the simple joys. And those must be countless.

O Lord, it's good to be among people. For me at least, the joy of people *does* exceed the disappointment and pain. And I am happy with people. And I thank you for us.

Amen.

People My Age Are Dying

Lately more people my age seem to be dying. Is that really the case or am I just being oversensitive?

Last week someone else died; it happened suddenly while he was playing tennis. Just a month ago another person died of a coronary while fixing breakfast at home.

What am I supposed to make of this? What is the point of it all if we're going to be cut down by "natural causes" right in the middle of life? I know we're not immortal, but this is something else.

Life is precious, God; certainly you know that. Why does it have to be so fragile? Why can't there be some way to insure it so that it doesn't get wiped out in one fleeting breath? Why can't it be beautiful without being delicate?

I don't know if this makes any sense to you; I'm not even sure it makes sense to me. All I know is this whole business is very disturbing.

Amen.

Why Isn't My Work the Fun
It Used to Be?

Why isn't my work the fun it used to be? What has happened to change that? I can't put my finger on it, God, because there are so many factors. Maybe it's just the inevitable passing of time; things do change and work doesn't remain static. Values shift, attitudes alter. What was "bottom line" yesterday is hardly considered today; what was peripheral before is dead center now.

Or maybe it's the people. People come and go. Maybe people used to be different than they are now; I'm sure they were. Maybe their expectations are different. Maybe they expect more of me, or less of me. They could be envious of me, or they could wonder how I ever got to doing what I'm doing.

Maybe it's just the environment, the atmosphere, the attitude. Or it may not be the external factors at all. Maybe it's an internal issue, or two or three.

Could I be bored—tired of doing what I've done for so many years? Is it a matter of dissatisfaction? Do I want more responsibility—less responsibility? Maybe I want to be doing something altogether different. Maybe I don't want to be doing anything at all. Possibly I'm over the hill, and I don't want to see that. Or perhaps it isn't even work that's the problem. Maybe it's something else in my life that I don't want to face, and work is a convenient scapegoat for the projection.

I don't know why my work isn't the fun it used to be. All I know is that it isn't. Please, God, help me in this with your firm support and give me a sense of direction. Whichever way I go please lead me toward a resolution and greater happiness and fulfillment.

Amen.

Children Seem to Grow Up Overnight

Why do children have to grow up so quickly? Do you play some sort of trick on us in terms of time when it comes to this experience? It seems we have kids and we go about our business, and there is nothing extraordinary about the passing of time; a day is a day and a year is a year.

But then all of a sudden, it has happened. And it *is* all of a sudden. People the world over have said so for ages. It is a universal truth: *children grow up overnight.*

I know there is no reliving the past, and I suppose that is what makes me melancholy. I don't think I have been a particularly bad parent, but when I look back in time I see the many lost opportunities that can never be recovered.

Will the true love that I feel for them and have honestly always felt for them, will that love cover a multitude of sins of omission?

O God, I hope so.

Amen.

My Life Is Like a Thunderstorm

I felt you this morning in the thunderstorm. In the exploding brilliance of light and sound I felt the awesome magnitude of your power. Lightning crackled among the clouds and reached a finger down to touch the ground a few miles off; it illuminated the earth with at least a billion candle-power. Seconds after, shattering crashes of thunder ripped through the sky, then roared and rumbled and groaned into silence . . . only to be followed by another splitting blast. The wind whipped and thrashed at the trees and small branches simply quit holding on and let go. The driving rain drenched everything in its path and had a smell of electricity about it.

I sat watching, hearing, and feeling the storm, God. And it occurred to me that this is not a bad analogy to my life right now. In fact, I find myself fairly often thinking that my life is very much like this storm.

If I felt you in the midst of this morning's thunderstorm, can I feel you in the center of my own storms?

I know your answer.

Amen.

What Opportunities Have I Missed?

I got to wondering again today, Lord. What opportunities have I missed in my years of living? How many "knocks at the door" did I fail to hear? How many "chances" passed by me that I didn't even see? What might I have been or done?

Then I got to thinking about how different things might have been had I been more self-confident when I was younger. What if I had been more willing to take a chance instead of playing it safe? If only I had had then the savvy and sophistication I seem to have now. What did my idealism cost me?

These are tough questions, Lord. Maybe they're dumb ones too. They seem to come mostly when I am down or discouraged or doubting myself. That's when I get to wondering. I don't think I am particularly dissatisfied or unhappy. Although, maybe I am. And I know it does no good to ruminate over the past. History is history; what has been, is.

But still I wonder. And the wondering does annoy me.

Amen.

I Don't Have Enough Time

Why am I continually running out of time? Why is it so different from when I was a child? When I was a child there was plenty of time. In fact, time often moved so slowly that it hardly seemed to move at all. I never even gave it much thought. Maybe I believed there was plenty of time and consequently didn't really care about it. Maybe I shouldn't care about time now, and it would pass more slowly. I doubt it.

You don't have this problem, do you, Lord? What is time to you? You are out of time, and yet you are in time. Do you know what it's like not to have enough time? It's terrible. And when you don't have enough time most of the time, it's worse than terrible.

Will it get better? Will the situation improve in the future? Can you help me somehow to be a little less distressed by my lack of time? Can you help me somehow to be a little better able to live with the time I have?

Amen.

You Give Us the Gift of Love

Love. O God you give us mortals the gift of love in all its splendor. The way of a man with a woman —a woman with a man: quietly intimate—fiercely passionate; sensuous—sacred; encompassing—penetrating; earthy—spiritual; excitingly ecstatic—and ever so gentle.

Deepen our love, God. Enrich it in our lives. Let us walk hand in hand with this thing called love, that we might know more the fullness and the abundance of life as you meant it.

Amen.

There's Sun above Those Clouds

The big silver bird rests quietly at the end of the long runway. It is hazy, very hazy, and the overcast is thick. The pilot has the brakes on, and as he revs up the jets, the plane, held in place by the brakes, begins to tremble gently. The feel of power is strong. The pilot eases off the brakes and the plane begins to thrust forward. Faster and faster it goes. And then it is off the ground and the thrill of takeoff overcomes me. We rise at a sharp angle and the lift is exhilarating. The fog and clouds whiz by as we plunge through the dense overcast. And then suddenly the brilliant sun, in all its magnificent splendor, bursts over the layer of clouds and floods the cabin with pure gold. And I am so moved inside that my eyes mist and I smile at the sun and say, "Thank you."

O God, my God, I know you are there even though I cannot see you. Above and beyond the darkness of these days your brilliance continues with uninterrupted clarity. Raise me O God; please lift my spirit. And like the big silver bird let me fly into your brightness.

Amen.

Where Does My Journey Take Me?

Where am I led? Where does my journey, my pilgrimage take me? Sometimes I feel so lost—my compass is misplaced and my sense of direction is badly disoriented. I thought I knew where I was headed and how I would get there. Have I been pulling the wool over my own eyes as well as deluding everyone else for all these years? I wonder.

Some of the "stuff" of my life, which I thought was firmly nailed down, seems to be coming loose, and it's scary. I can no longer move ahead in well-traveled ruts with an ease and confidence that is the envy of others. Somehow it is all more serious now, and indeed more complicated. My sophisticated certainty has proved more superficial than in-depth. So now it becomes clear to me that finding one's way demands of us more than many of us want to realize.

But you are a guide, Lord, a willing guide. I know that; in fact, I've known it all along. Please walk with me as you have said you would, and help me on my journey.

Amen.

I See Opportunity
in the Midst of Turmoil

It certainly is a time of turmoil and distress. In fact, I'd be hard pressed to find any portion of my life that isn't literally "up for grabs" in this transition. But what amazes me is that in the midst of it all I can see opportunity. Actually, I think there are more open doors now than ever before in my life.

That's surprising; yet I guess it really isn't. You seem to have made us so that our vision gets sharper as our situations become more perilous. I don't know, maybe that's an overstatement, but that's the way it often feels to me. Here I am seeming to wander aimlessly through this maze of mid-life and I discover possibilities for my life that before were beyond even my consideration.

I'm not sure how that comes about, but I rejoice that it does and I thank you for it. It is good to have holes in the cloud cover through which the sun can shine.

Amen.

I'm Balancing Cynicism and Gratitude

Some days it would be very easy to become an outright cynic. With no trouble at all I could write off the whole human race, or at least the vast majority of it. People seem to have lost common sense and common courtesy. Oh, sure, there are notable exceptions, but by and large people don't seem to care much about other people. People *say* they care, but they don't even know what the word means. Politicians running for office say they "care" when they're only interested in getting elected. Businesses advertise that they "care" when all they're interested in is getting your money. People who supposedly "care" don't even pay attention to what you're saying when you are conversing with them (if you can call it that).

Still, in spite of all that, there is a kind of balance that seems to slip into my living of these days, Lord. Not that there isn't plenty to complain about, but there does seem to be an awful lot for which to be grateful. I don't think I'm anywhere near being ready to abandon my cynicism, but on the other hand, gratitude is more a part of my experience than ever before. I don't know if I have particularly cultivated it or if it's just that I *feel* gratitude. I am aware of being grateful. Taking things in life for granted seems to be less the case for me, and I'm more ready to express thanks.

Please help me not to lose that dimension, Lord. I know I will still live with my complaining nature, but gratitude and graciousness are very desirable. And I suspect that you aren't too upset with those qualities either.

Amen.

Parenting Can Be Maddening

What a struggle it is; what a horrendous struggle! I think that any parent who makes it through rearing kids, who allows them to develop as themselves should be granted some special degree of sainthood. Kids can drive a parent totally berserk. Why can't they see things the way I see them? Why can't they perform and behave and act as I would want?

It is maddening—that's the word—maddening. And I need help. I need help to continue to accept them as the unique persons they are, because that is truly what I want to do. I need help to keep from molding them into reproductions of myself. I need help to nourish the qualities that are theirs. I need help to stop myself from throwing my hands in the air and screaming, "Oh, do what you want to do; I just don't care!" Because I *do* care; you know how much I love them.

O God, dear God, please give me the wisdom and the patience to walk that thin line between being overresponsible and irresponsible. Lead me to give them freedom within limits. Help me to model for them and then to trust their ability to discern. And help *them* finally to forgive my shortcomings and my mistakes.

Amen.

My Spouse Has Changed

This is not a complaint, Lord; I simply want to make an observation. My wife is not the woman I married. Furthermore she tells me that I am not the man she married. People *do* change; we are not statically fixated at some point in life—namely our wedding day. So it is reasonable; but it is also unreasonable. It is good; but it is also not good. It is pleasing; but it is also very threatening.

Where do we go from here, we married strangers? What shall we do with the emerging newness, the "differentness" in each other? Celebrate? Or try to return the status quo? Celebration sounds like a lot more fun, but I suspect it is also the scarier of the options. To rejoice in a potentially new life in each other, to support and encourage new facets of our beings, to redevelop a relationship of 20-some years—what will it mean? What will be the consequences?

Courage and acceptance are what we seem to need, Lord. Not courage to run away from or avoid or reject this "newness of life," this "change" in us, but courage to view this as an opportunity, and the ability to accept it as an opportunity for positive consequence.

I suspect this is going to take some time. So please walk with me—walk with both of us—through this stretch of our journey, and give us an abundance of patience and empathy, and above all, love.

Amen.

I Don't Like Criticism

I have decided that I don't take criticism very easily. But then, who does? On the one hand, I tell myself I am not that influenced by what other people think or do not think of me, but on the other hand, I want people to think well of me, and I don't like it when they are critical or unsupportive.

Some people say that when someone criticizes you it doesn't necessarily mean that the person doesn't like you. Well, I'll tell you, Lord, that sounds good rationally and academically, but on the feeling level it's pretty hard to separate the two. I may know intellectually that there is some truth to that, but in actual experience I don't handle it very well. It is so much more comfortable, satisfying, and fulfilling when there is acceptance and agreement.

Oh, yes, I know full well that all this is just an old, warmed-over struggle with perfectionism. And I know that because of my imperfection, criticism and disagreement are inevitable. And I even know that that is really okay—I am not going to be devastated and perish. Consequently I get somewhat annoyed with myself whenever I get into this thing. But I still don't take criticism very easily, God. Who does?
Amen.

I Don't Think
I Would Ever Do Myself In

I heard about another attempted suicide today. The person almost succeeded. He has recovered from the attempt but he'll be disabled for the rest of his life—however long that is.

I don't think I would ever commit suicide. At least I don't *think* so. Not that I haven't thought about it, and thought about how I might do it if I were going to do it. The thought has only occurred to me when I have been in deepest despair, especially when life has seemed overwhelming and when I've felt sorry for myself and sorry for the plight I've found myself in.

But there is always a way out, isn't there, God? I can believe that. No matter how deep the despair, there is always a way out besides killing myself. You give us a thing called hope. You assure us and reassure us that whatever our situation, there is hope. And that is not an artificial palliative but something very real.

O God, when I walk through my shadowy valleys, hold fast to me in my despair and let me feel your hand in mine. Let hope never be lost to my eyes and let my courage be strengthened by your power.

Amen.

There Is Too Much Injustice

I certainly wish you would exercise your authority. If vengeance is yours, how about going after it? You are letting people get away with murder. The Bible tells stories about how you used to intervene—how you literally had a hand in the affairs of this world. Well, I'll tell you, now things are just as bad, if not worse, than they were then, so where are you?

It's just not fair. Justice, where it exists, is twisted and perverted. The Old Testament psalmists ranted and raved about how the wicked prospered while those who tried to do what was right got nothing but pain and suffering. Well, it really hasn't changed very much, you know. In fact it seems like it's worse than ever.

What's the incentive for trying to be a just person? I'd say there is precious little, if any. Having to be mean and aggressive just so you aren't abused is a sad commentary on the way life has evolved.

I don't really know what I expect you to do. But you have *got* to know how fed up I am with the injustice that is going on.

Amen.

I'm Proud of Our Children

We got together for the holiday. Those who had "flown the nest" returned. The coming together was joyful; the celebrating was satisfying and fulfilling. But perhaps more than anything else I was aware of a feeling of pride—pride in our children who are maturing into sensitive and responsible people. They are turning out to be "good apples," and I thank you very much for that. I am so very proud of them.

There never is a guarantee, and that's what makes it risky. We worked hard and did what we believed was right, and we hoped a lot, and you know we prayed a lot, but there was never a guarantee that they would not turn out to be bad apples. But they didn't, and I rejoice in that.

I had a good, deep feeling as I looked across the table at them—a feeling of pride in them and humble gratitude to you.

Amen.

Has Life Passed Me By?

Lord, I think in many ways life has passed me by. So many times I look around me, and I realize that I missed a lot of living in my earlier years. There were so many things that I might have done then and didn't do. There were so many things I *couldn't* do. I suppose I lived through the experiences with a kind of "sour grapes" rationalization—coping with undesirable reality, wishing it might be otherwise, but knowing better.

I still wish it might have been otherwise, and I regret it somehow. It's a kind of melancholy feeling, Lord. I wish I had done this or done that when I was younger because now it's too late—either the desire or the physical strength is gone—and I feel sad because what never was can never be, and I've lost the experience forever.

Oh yes, there is plenty of contentment in my life, but today the discontent is strong, and the regrets are heavy on me. Maybe tomorrow will be better.

Amen.

I'm Sick Today

I'm sick and I don't feel much like talking. Yet I still want to. I seem to fall ill more easily nowadays. It's nothing really serious—I just seem to go down under every passing bug. Maybe my resistance is weakening with my advancing years. Or maybe I'm more vulnerable because I use up all my energy dealing with all the miserable stresses that plague me. What do you think? Is it possible that I'm even using illness to avoid some of the reality I don't want to face?

Whatever the case, I wish you would help my health to improve. I didn't used to be this way, and it's very distressing.

Amen.

There's Security in Insecurity

I suspect you get tired of hearing me talk about this, but if you don't want to hear it then you shouldn't have encouraged us to be open and up front with you.

When is it going to level off? Notice I'm not asking, "When am I going to be done with this business?" I'm simply inquiring, "When is it going to *level off*?" Is there ever going to be some kind of resolution of all these conflicts within me, or am I destined to live forever with the tension and feel the pull of opposites inside me? I think my life is one big bundle of contradictions, and I wonder if I'm ever going to regain any sense of balance.

Still, somehow I sense a dimension of peace and serenity beneath it all. I don't think it's some kind of self-hypnosis. It's a real foundation for my life imbedded in you. I don't even understand what that means. All I know is that there is some kind of security in my insecurity and some kind of certitude in all my uncertainty. And you are responsible for that. And I thank you.

Amen.

My Spirituality Has Changed

I'm very much aware that my spirituality isn't the same as it was in the first half of life, Lord. Maybe it's more nontraditional and less stereotypical, more practical and less theoretical, more urgent and less passive.

I am still moved to great depths when standing inside those magnificent European cathedrals, tilting my head back farther and farther, following the splendorous arches as they stretch to touch the very footstool of heaven. And I am stirred by the choir's Gregorian chants echoing gently in the holy stillness.

Oh, yes, there is so much of tradition that does and will forever proclaim the message, "God is!" But I must also add that I believe I see you and feel you more outside the structure called the church than I do within.

My dear God, I have come to a point in my life where being fed the pap of party line platitudes generates only depression. Euphemisms, however zealously proclaimed, are only that. And where people balk at giving one another a simple greeting in your house, mouthed commitment to *agape* love is an offense.

I need something solid that will help me wrestle with the issues of my life. I need someone who isn't afraid to say, "I don't know," whose authenticity will convict my foolishness and graciously raise my spirit. I need someone to identify with me and em-

brace me without embarrassment or thought of reward.

All this is just another one of my conflicts, Lord.
But somehow I am more at peace in the midst of this
particular struggle.

Amen.

Why Am I in Such a Bind?

Every once in a while I wonder why I feel so miserably upset about my life. Then I begin to feel guilty about my concern over my lot in life. After all, life is really not all that bad. Why should I feel so distressed? Why shouldn't I rejoice and be grateful for what is? Why shouldn't I be more thankful and content? Why should I perceive my life as one of turmoil when there probably are more people who envy me than pity me?

Is this all part of my confusion? Is this all part of my ambiguity and my vascillation? Is this a demonstration of the contradictions that seem to tug away at me in a kind of violent warfare? O God, I just don't know. But then again I *do* know. Every bit of it is true and authentic. This is my bind.

I hope it is okay to be in this kind of a bind because that certainly is where I am. You know how truly grateful I am for what I have achieved and what I have acquired. But that isn't the point, is it? And that is why these quarrels within myself are really exercises in futility.

What I need is your good guidance to rejoice in the good things while I suffer the pain of the not so good. I need to realize that each is going to continually invade the other. There really is no total good or total evil, is there? Help me to celebrate the good, knowing it has its minuses. And help me to suffer the not so good, hoping for its potential pluses.

Amen.

Help Me Act and Not Just Wish

Have you ever noticed how many "wishers" there are around? I mean those of us who "wish I could do this" or "would like to do that." We seem to live in a kind of controlled existence that disallows our using the talents and resources that you give to us. Time and time again we repeat those phrases so that history and present and future get all blended into one powerless glob.

There are plenty of things that I wish I could have done or would surely have liked to have done in the past. But all that is history, and there is absolutely nothing I can do about that, except to let it be my continuing guide. And that is precisely what far too many of us do, God. We go on saying, "Oh yes, I really would like to do that," and never go any farther.

I am convinced that a healthy portion of my dissatisfaction in life is the result of lack of direction. I hear myself say, "I really ought to do this" or "I really would like to do that," and I rarely see action following those phrases. But, God, when I decide, "This is what I want to do," I go on and do it—I get where I have decided I will go.

I know my laziness is a great enemy—it is so much less work to say "I wish" rather than to make concrete plans and set achievable goals. So please give me your guidance and support, and encourage me to chart my course rather than be swept along by any passing current. Bless me with an eye of vision and dream and the strength to bring them into reality.

Amen.

People Can Be a Pain in the Neck

I really do like people, but sometimes they get
on my nerves so much that I think I'll go crazy. I
just want to get away from them. Some people suffer such whining paranoia that they make you think
the fates have chosen them personally to receive the
agonies reserved only for the damned. Others must
lie awake at night concocting ways to deliberately
mess up their lives. They must go *out of their way*
to create their miseries.

No wonder Jesus went off into the wilderness so
often by himself. He was up against the same thing,
wasn't he? He knew full well that he had to get away
from people from time to time. But the time to be
away was renewing. And maybe, dear God, it
could be for me, too. Help me get away for awhile
to be with you, and in that solitude help me find
restoration.

Amen.

Am I Much of a Risk-Taker?

I discovered something, Lord. It dawned on me that I am not nearly the risk-taker I always thought I was. As a matter of fact, I have played it pretty safe over the years. I think I abandoned risk taking when I turned 18. Of course there are risks and then there are *risks*. I guess the pre-18 risks were probably foolhardy episodes—flirtations with serious trouble.

But looking back over the years since I was 18, I have to conclude that I played it rather safe. I became and did pretty much what was expected of me. That is especially amusing to me, Lord, because I have liked very much to consider myself a true taker of risks and an encourager of others to do likewise.

This discovery is surprising and even amusing, but it is also disconcerting. I wonder if I'm missing the "abundant life" you spoke of.

Amen.

Will I Have a Happy Ending?

No doubt this is going to sound like a foolish question, but, could you tell me, am I going to have a happy ending? I'm not even sure I know what I mean by that, and it really isn't that I'm curious about details. I just wonder, am I going to have a happy ending?

I wouldn't say I am preoccupied with endings, but I do seem to be giving *my* ending more consideration than ever before in my life. I have seen so many unhappy endings—and continue to see them—that I've begun to wonder about mine. It seems there are so many variables and the possibility of so many unexpected factors—you know, "The best laid plans of mice and men," etc.

I think I know how to go about providing as best I can for a happy ending, but I also know that I have only so much control over the future—my future. And will I even make the "right" decisions about what I control?

Even now I am unsure. I say to myself, "Are you being wise or are you a fool? Is your hanging on or letting go working towards happiness or anguish in the end? When do you play safe and when do you risk?"

O God, I know you won't give me an answer to my question. Only I can live out the answer. But what you can give me is courage, please, and faith that I might move on with a degree of certainty towards my ending. Let me have trust and let me have hope that happiness will indeed be. But most of all, let me have you . . . your touch . . . your hand.

   Amen.

The Simple Is Really Very Desirable

A fellow criticized me the other day for being too simplistic. I had been talking about handling stress, and I suggested that a very helpful habit was to remember the phrase, "This too will pass." He thought that was much too naive and impotent. And who knows, perhaps he's right.

Maybe it *is* an oversimplification, but I have decided that I prefer the simple to the complex. I greatly admire people who can take the very complex and simplify it so that I can get the drift of it.

You did that, God, didn't you? You took the most complex of all and made it simple enough for a child to grasp. Unfathomably complex, you simplified yourself to become one of us. Who but you would have thought to do that? Who but you would have had the security to do that?

A simple man from beginning to end—Jesus. Master of all universes and God of all gods—Jesus. An unbelievable equation, but true. An inexplicable occurrence, but true. Too preposterous to have merit, but true.

Thank you, O Lord God Almighty, for the simple. Amen.

When I Get to Feeling Abused

I had the urge again, Lord, just to give it all up and go off by myself somewhere. Who needs all this hassle anyway? I do and do and do, and for what? Who really cares? Everyone is looking out for number one. Everyone wants his or her own way. It's alright for me to do for others, but for them to do for me without my asking them or telling them—forget it.

I really don't think the payoff is worth the cost. It's an uphill struggle all the way. I feel so alone I might as well *be* alone—it certainly would be a lot less struggle. People get so caught up in taking things for granted that they lose sight of what it costs others to provide for them. Where is the gratitude?

I think I could be a lot better off. Emotional demands would be less; I wouldn't have to be so responsible and accountable; I could actually spend for myself for a change.

It's just that I begin to feel that I keep on giving and rarely get. Have you ever felt like that, Lord?

Amen.

What Can I / Can't I Control?

I have come upon an interesting observation about myself, Lord. It's a kind of inconsistency (among many others I have noticed) that is both amusing and troublesome. I complain about not being able to control those things that are impossible to control, while at the same time I fail to control those things that I *can* control.

I know I would much rather have my way than not have my way. Still I know that I *cannot* always have my own way. I *know* that intellectually, but I still find myself emotionally desiring and even expecting it. So when I'm up against that which I cannot in any way control, I still want to control it, and I get angry and resentful because I can't. I want my way.

But when it comes to those things over which I *can* have control, I often find myself doing the "powerless" number, saying, "Oh, I can't do that," or "I can't do anything about that," and avoiding or projecting personal responsibility.

Is it plain and simply human perversity to go for the easiest road? I guess it is. In your wisdom, though, you allow us to take occasional glimpses into ourselves and see these perversions and realize that we can do something about them if we wish. But whether or not I will take control of that, God, I just don't know. I will really need your help on this one.
Amen.

I Don't Seem to Sleep As Well

"Now I lay me down to sleep." And then I add, "If only I could." If only I could lie down and just go to sleep. I used to be able to do that. Now I lie down and a thousand different things race through my mind. I don't seem to be at peace—peace in which I can drop off to sleep. All I do is think about this and wonder about that and sort and shuffle the events of my life. My mind seems to be on a constant go, and it is exasperating and exhausting.

What is the matter with me, Lord? It isn't that I worry—at least I don't think I'm worrying. It isn't that I don't have faith and trust—I believe I really do. It's just a feeling of uncertainty and a whole new reassessment of what I am and what I am about. It bothers me because I seem to be the only one troubled by this, and those in whom I confide just seem to brush it aside as of little consequence.

O God, I really am tired. Will this soon pass so that I can return to some degree of normalcy?

Amen.

There Is a Joy in Mellowing

The passing of time does have a way of mellowing one, God. That undoubtedly is one of the benefits of moving into the second half of life. "Catastrophies" are fewer; "the end of the world" occurs less frequently; I keep my cool and calm more often than ever before. I am discovering that many things are not all that important. Oh, many are, certainly; but many more disturbances or upsets, I am discovering, can be taken in stride and dealt with without a corresponding elevation in blood pressure. It is frankly a much more satisfying and pleasant way to live.

I am afraid I have taken life much too seriously for far too long. And I rejoice that at this point I am able to relax my hold on my life and let it slip around in my fingers a little more freely. You don't give us enough years to live them compulsively in "dead earnest." And so we must step back, mustn't we, and smile at ourselves regularly, laugh at ourselves periodically, and even on occasion belt out a raucous guffaw.

Thank you for the abundant life. I'm glad I finally found another dimension of it.

Amen.

Decision Making Is Difficult

It would have been a lot easier for us all if you hadn't decided to give us a free will and the power of choice. I'm sure you know that. In fact I would suspect that you yourself may even have had an occasional second thought about the wisdom of your decision. Granted, it gives us a tremendous amount of freedom, but all that freedom can sometimes be pretty scary.

Somehow this must be affecting me because lately I seem to be wishing more often that I didn't have to make decisions—that somehow things would work themselves out without my having to take a position and bear the responsibility of that decision. If I'm going to bear the responsibility that freedom of choice demands, I'm going to have to have courage to make my decisions and live out their consequences. I know that very well. What troubles me is that I seem lately to have less courage and greater hesitancy than ever before.

Is this simply another part of moving into the second half of life? Will it improve? Will I regain my self-confidence? I don't understand it; I am probably more self-confident now than ever before in my life, and yet. . . .

Please let me feel your support beneath my weakness.

Amen.

I Find Solitude Appealing

These moments of communion with you are precious, God. The silence and the separation are very satisfying. Solitude has become very appealing to me, and to commune with you or with myself is refreshing.

I am surprised at this appeal; it is another new facet of my being that has come so clearly into focus. To be away from others, to be by myself, to experience the solitude of aloneness is quite contrary to my extravertive nature. But I have found its rewards to be deep and many, and I cherish it.

Let me feel your closeness in my meditations; let me know you hear the ramblings of my prayers. Give me courage to possess what I discover in myself. Seek me in my solitude, and let me find you.

Amen.

My God, You Are the Song of My Heart

O God, my God, there is truly none but you. No matter what I may say or how I may behave, no matter how contradictory my life may be or how utterly extraordinary the words may sound, in the depth of my heart of hearts you are my all, my everything. I am destroyed by the awesomeness of your power; I am raised by the splendor of your beauty. You stir cosmic storms into holocausts; you sear the sky with a blaze of sunset; you paint mountains and canyons with a stroke of your finger; and you give beautiful music to a bird whose value is half a penny.

And you choose, O mighty, holy God, you choose to look on me with favor. You willingly choose to bless me. You invade me and pervade me, yet all the while you respect the person I am—the person you chose to give me. It is all too wonderful for me that this should be; yet am I bold enough to claim it as mine.

Oh, loving God, you who indeed *are* my all, fill me with your good Spirit as I walk the journey of my years. This extraordinary time is a zenith in my pilgrimage, laden with changes and questions and uncertainties and fears, but likewise pregnant with new and abundant life and unimaginable potential.

Please walk the path with me, and that shall be all I need.

Amen.